WRITTEN BY JOE SULLIVAN    DESIGNED BY JON DALRYMPLE

A Grange Publication

© 2023. Published by Grange Communications Ltd., Edinburgh, under licence from Celtic Football Club. Printed in the EU.

Photographs by Alan Whyte and Ryan Whyte, Angus Johnston, Celtic Multi-Media, SNS, Alamy.

Champions Artwork by Shaun Campbell, Robert Mackenzie.

Celtic logo is a registered trademark of The Celtic Football Club.

ISBN 978-1-915879-14-1

# CONTENTS

# BRENDAN

**CELTIC kicked-off season 2023/24 having won no fewer than SEVENTEEN of the previously available 21 domestic trophies in Scottish top-level football, and the man who kick-started that phenomenal run was back at Paradise.**

Brendan Rodgers first arrived at Celtic Park as manager in 2016 and promised to fill the area of the upper-seating deck that had been closed.

He said at the time: "I grew up seeing Celtic Park full and I know in the last couple of years, the top tier of the Lisbon Lions' Stand has been shut. We need to get it reopened, get people back in there and get this stadium back going."

He did more than fulfil his promise to fill the stadium, he also filled the trophy cabinet with alarming regularity – alarming for others outside Celtic that is – as his first term in charge delivered an unprecedented Invincible Treble with the Hoops going through the entire domestic season unbeaten in all three competitions.

The manager followed that up with an 'unprecedented' – there's that word again – second successive Treble in 2017/18 and, prior to departing in early 2019, he added the League Cup once more to take his personal tally to seven tournaments entered and seven trophies won.

We could use words like unparalleled or unmatched, but 'unprecedented' was the buzzword for the Celtic of the late 2010s and on into the current decade with those seven trophies being added to by another **TEN**. Not only was the club's second nine-in-a-row reached, another two Trebles gave us the previously unbelievable Quadruple Treble with Celtic winning all 12 available trophies successively as the manager's fellow Irishman, Neil Lennon took up the baton.

When he was replaced by Ange Postecoglou, the silverware just kept on coming with the Australian winning five out of six competitions entered and he finished off with the players delivering the club's fifth Treble in just seven seasons for a remarkable world record of **EIGHT** Trebles.

All of this was started by Brendan Rodgers. When he arrived, the club had won three Trebles and 99 major trophies. His first ever silverware, the League Cup with Celtic was the club's 100th trophy – that he returned after a relatively short period to a club that now had 116 trophies and the world record for Trebles speaks volumes as to Celtic's standing in modern football, and the Irishman was crucial as a keystone to all that was to follow.

He is now back at Paradise as manager once more, and he and everyone else at the club are intent on maintaining that standing and standard set by Celtic.

# RODGERS

## MANAGER FACTFILE

D.O.B: 26/01/73
Born: Carnlough, Ireland

### PLAYING CAREER RECORD

Ballymena United (1987-90)
Reading (1990-93)
Newport (1993-94)
Witney Town (1994-95)
Newbury Town (1995-96)

### MANAGERIAL HONOURS

**CELTIC:**

League Champions
(2016/17, 2017/18)

Scottish Cup Winners
(2016/17, 2017/18)

League Cup Winners
(2016/17, 2017/18, 2018/19)

**LEICESTER CITY:**

FA Cup
(2020/21)

FA Community Shield
(2021)

### AS MANAGER

| | |
|---|---|
| Watford | (2008-09) |
| Reading | (2009) |
| Swansea City | (2010-12) |
| Liverpool | (2012-15) |
| Celtic | (2016-19) |
| Leicester City | (2019-23) |
| Celtic | (2023 to date) |

### CLUB HONOURS

**Scottish League Winners [53 times]**

1892/93, 1893/94, 1895/96, 1897/98, 1904/05,
1905/06, 1906/07, 1907/08, 1908/09, 1909/10,
1913/14, 1914/15,1915/16, 1916/17, 1918/19,
1921/22, 1925/26, 1935/36, 1937/38, 1953/54,
1965/66, 1966/67, 1967/68, 1968/69, 1969/70,
1970/71, 1971/72, 1972/73, 1973/74, 1976/77,
1978/79, 1980/81, 1981/82, 1985/86, 1987/88,
1997/98, 2000/01, 2001/02, 2003/04, 2005/06,
2006/07, 2007/08, 2011/12, 2012/13, 2013/14,
2014/15, 2015/16, 2016/17, 2017/18, 2018/19,
2019/20, 2021/22, 2022/23.

**Scottish Cup Winners [41 times]**

1892, 1899, 1900, 1904, 1907, 1908, 1911, 1912,
1914, 1923, 1925, 1927, 1931, 1933, 1937, 1951,
1954, 1965, 1967, 1969, 1971, 1972, 1974, 1975,
1977, 1980, 1985, 1988, 1989, 1995, 2001, 2004,
2005, 2007, 2011, 2013, 2017, 2018, 2019, 2020,
2023

**League Cup Winners [21 times]**

1956/57, 1957/58, 1965/66, 1966/67, 1967/68,
1968/69, 1969/70, 1974/75, 1982/83, 1997/98,
1999/00, 2000/01, 2005/06, 2008/09, 2014/15,
2016/17, 2017/18, 2018/19, 2019/20, 2021/22.
2022/23

**European Cup Winners 1967**

**Coronation Cup Winners 1953**

**Treble Winners (8 Times)**

1966/67, 1968/69, 2000/01, 2016/17, 2017/18,
2018/19, 2019/20, 2022/23

# CELTIC'S CENTURY NETBUSTERS

## HISTORY-MAKING CELTS FIRING ON ALL CYLINDERS

**KYOGO'S 27 league goals in 2022/23 helped the Hoops to one of their best ever title tallies in what was also one of the club's quickest seasons for reaching the century goalscoring mark.**

This was the first time since the league split was introduced in season 2000/01 that the 100-goal tally was attained before the top six/bottom six divide was reached at the 33-game mark.

Here are some facts and figures from the record-breaking free-scoring Celts.

Celtic breached the 100-league goal tally for the 2022/23 term – a feat managed by the Celts on 10 previous occasions, the first time in season 1915/16, and the most recent being 2016/17 when the Celts reached 106 goals. This time they topped that by netting an incredible 114 league goals.

In all competitions, the Celts scored 147 goals with the 114 league goals being added to by 12 in the League Cup, 17 in the Scottish Cup and four in the UEFA Champions League.

This was the first time that a century of goals had been reached by any team before the league split. The tally was reached and bypassed in the 4-1 win over Kilmarnock at Rugby Park on April 16 that took the Celts to 102 goals. This was the 32nd game of the campaign with another game still to play before the split. The 100th goal was scored by Daizen Maeda.

The Hoops scored an average of exactly three goals per game during the league campaign, and repeated the feat of the Celts in the 1937/38 title win when the side also scored 114 goals in 38 games.

Celtic's highest-scoring league campaign was the 116 goals from 38 games in season 1915/16 for an average of 3.05 goals per game, while the lowest average from the 11 century-scoring campaigns is 2.66 goals per game from the 101 scored in 38 games in season 1930/31.

The Hoops have also breached the 100-goal mark in three consecutive seasons – Jock Stein's first three full terms in charge as 106 goals in 1965/66 and 1967/68 sandwiched the 111 goals scored by the Celts in the all-conquering season of 1966/67.

Those 111 league goals scored in the Lisbon season actually delivered the best average of 3.26 goals per game as they were scored in only 34 games that term, four fewer than the current 38 – indeed all three consecutive 100-goal campaigns by Jock Stein's side were only 34 games long.

## REACHING 100 LEAGUE GOALS

| Season | Date | Game No. | Goals/Games | Ratio |
|--------|------|----------|-------------|-------|
| 1915/16 | April 15 | 33rd game | 116 goals in 38 games | 3.05 goals per game |
| 2022/23 | April 16 | 32nd game | 114 goals in 38 games | 3.00 goals per game |
| 1937/38 | April 10 | 34th game | 114 goals in 38 games | 3.00 goals per game |
| 1966/67 | March 27 | 29th game | 111 goals in 34 games | 3.26 goals per game |
| 1965/66 | April 9 | 30th game | 106 goals in 34 games | 3.12 goals per game |
| 1967/68 | April 12 | 32nd game | 106 goals in 34 games | 3.12 goals per game |
| 2016/17 | May 18 | 37th game | 106 goals in 38 games | 2.79 goals per game |
| 2003/04 | April 25 | 34th game | 105 goals in 38 games | 2.76 goals per game |
| 2013/14 | May 11 | 38th game | 102 goals in 38 games | 2.68 goals per game |
| 1930/31 | April 25 | 37th game | 101 goals in 38 games | 2.66 goals per game |
| 1926/27 | April 30 | 38th game | 101 goals in 38 games | 2.66 goals per game |

## THE MEN WHO NETTED 114 LEAGUE GOALS IN ONE SEASON

| | | | |
|---|---|---|---|
| Kyogo | 27 | David Turnbull | 4 |
| Jota | 11 | Matt O'Riley | 3 |
| Liel Abada | 10 | Carl Starfelt | 3 |
| Daizen Maeda | 8 | Greg Taylor | 3 |
| Reo Hatate | 6 | Moritz Jenz | 2 |
| Hyeongyu Oh | 6 | Alexandro Bernabei | 1 |
| Giorgos Giakoumakis | 6 | Alistair Johnston | 1 |
| Sead Hakšabanović | 5 | Stephen Welsh | 1 |
| James Forrest | 4 | Josip Juranovic | 1 |
| Callum McGregor | 4 | Own Goals | 4 |
| Aaron Mooy | 4 | | |

# JULY

**WHEREAS seasons in recent years have seen the Hoops involved in European games as early as mid-July, there was a more than welcome bit of breathing space this term thanks to the Hoops qualifying directly for the group stages of the UEFA Champions League.**

There would also be a change to the usual schedule later on in the 2022/23 season thanks to the Qatar World Cup taking place in winter, resulting in a change to the December/January fixture list and mid-season break.

The result was that the Celts could prepare for the upcoming season with a variety of friendly outings before kicking off the brand-new season in earnest with Aberdeen visiting on the very last day of the month to mark the start of the new campaign for the champions.

Ange Postecoglou's side jetted out for the first batch of games, with Austria the location of the pre-season base camp while, over the course of the month, new arrivals included Ben Siegrist, Alexandro Bernabei and Aaron Mooy, whilst Moritz Jenz came in on loan. The biggest news of all was that Portuguese star, Jota had committed

himself to the Hoops by following in the footsteps of Cameron Carter-Vickers who had signed the previous month.

There were two games against Austrian opposition with a trip over the border to the Czech Republic before two friendlies at home against English opposition sandwiched a jaunt to Poland for Artur Boruc's tribute match, as the Hoops remained unbeaten in the six games before the arrival of Aberdeen for Flag Day.

Celtic skipper Callum McGregor carried the SPFL trophy out before unfurling the flag as the champions started the defence of their silverware with a win.

The final score was 2-0 but it could have been a whole lot more as Stephen Welsh got the first goal of the season after only three minutes. Jota celebrated his new contract in fine style with a very early contender for Goal of the Season to ensure the points would be staying at Celtic Park.

# HOOPS HIGHPOINT

When it comes to a highpoint, what better way to kick off a season than by paying tribute to just how successful you were the previous term, as that's what happened when Celtic skipper Callum McGregor unfurled the 2021/22 league flag. A win and a clean sheet only added to the occasion as the Celts kicked-off the defence of their title in fine style.

## THE GAMES

| Comp | Venue | Date | Opposition | Score | Scorers |
|------|-------|------|------------|-------|---------|
| FR | A | Wed 6 | Wiener Viktoria | 7-0 | Kenny 10 & 25, Hatate 13, Johnston 17, Jullien 43, Forrest 44, Vata 76 |
| FR | A | Sat 9 | Rapid Vienna | 3-3 | O'Riley 9, Turnbull 56, Kyogo 64 |
| FR | A | Wed 13 | Banik Ostrava | 4-2 | Kyogo 14, O'Riley 25, Giakoumakis 48, Abada 74 |
| FR | H | Sat 16 | Blackburn Rovers | 2-2 | Jota 16, Turnbull 27 |
| FR | A | Wed 20 | Legia Warsaw | 2-2 | Hatate 20, Maeda 42 |
| FR | H | Sat 23 | Norwich City | 2-0 | Maeda 35, Turnbull 67 |
| SPF | H | Sun 31 | Aberdeen | 2-0 | Welsh 3, Jota 75 |

## TOP OF THE TREE

| | P | W | D | L | F | A | GD | Pts |
|------|---|---|---|---|---|---|----|-----|
| 1 CELTIC | 1 | 1 | 0 | 0 | 2 | 0 | 2 | 3 |
| 2 Hearts | 1 | 1 | 0 | 0 | 2 | 1 | 1 | 3 |
| 3 Rangers | 1 | 1 | 0 | 0 | 2 | 1 | 1 | 3 |

# CELTIC 2022/2023 : MONTH BY MONTH
# AUGUST

THE first full competitive month of the term saw five games, and only one of them at home but with a magnificent aggregate score of 23-2 for the Hoops with Ross County being the only team to score against the Celts.

The highlight was an SPFL record-breaking 9-0 away win over Dundee United – equalling the 9-0 home win by the Celts over Aberdeen in 2010, and keeping a close eye on the proceedings at Tannadice was new Bhoy, Sead Hakšabanović who was the latest signing earlier that week.

The month was bookended with away wins over Ross County, one in the league and one in the League Cup for a 7-2 total in the trips to Dingwall, with Moritz Jenz netting his first Celtic goal in the opening game, and adding his next in the following game – a stylish 5-0 win over Kilmarnock at Rugby Park, with Carl Starfelt getting his first Hoops goal during the match.

## THE GAMES

| Comp | Venue | Date | Opposition | Score | Scorers |
|------|-------|------|-----------|-------|---------|
| SPFL | A | Sat 6 | Ross County | 3-1 | Kyogo 48, Jenz 84, Abada 90+1 |
| SPFL | A | Sun 14 | Kilmarnock | 5-0 | Kyogo 7, Jota 35, Jenz 46, Starfelt 76, Giakoumakis 82 |
| SPFL | H | Sun 21 | Hearts | 2-0 | Kyogo 13, Giakoumakis 94+4 |
| SPFL | A | Sun 28 | Dundee United | 9-0 | Kyogo 15, 40, 45+2, Jota 45+6, Abada 50, 59, 77, Juranovic 55, Starfelt 81 |
| LC | A | Wed 31 | Ross County | 4-1 | McGregor 21, Giakoumakis 25, Maeda 73, Forrest 90 |

## TOP OF THE TREE

| | P | W | D | L | F | A | GD | Pts |
|---|---|---|---|---|---|---|----|-----|
| 1 CELTIC | 5 | 5 | 0 | 0 | 21 | 1 | 20 | 15 |
| 2 Rangers | 5 | 4 | 1 | 0 | 14 | 3 | 11 | 13 |
| 3 Hearts | 5 | 3 | 1 | 1 | 10 | 7 | 3 | 10 |

# HOOPS HIGHPOINT

It's not often you get a 9-0 win, but it's also rare to have two hat-trick scorers in one game, and that's what happened when both Kyogo and Liel Abada both hit triples against Dundee United. It was Celtic's first double hat-trick since the previous 9-0 win when Gary Hooper and Anthony Stokes did so against Aberdeen in 2010 – both wins being record SPFL home and away wins. The Tannadice match was the 18th to feature a double hat-trick for Celtic, with the first being a 9-2 win over Clyde in 1888.

Another scorer in both of those matches was Kyogo, who kept that up over the first four games of the month and also netted a hat-trick in the 9-0 win at Tannadice along with Liel Abada, who likewise netted three times in that match.

In between those matches was the only Saturday game of the month when Hearts visited Celtic Park. The Hoops recorded a 2-0 win with Kyogo opening the scoring, but it wasn't until time added on that Giorgos Giakoumakis truly sealed the win.

There were a number of changes to the starters just a few days later as the Celts travelled back north, this time back to Dingwall for the League Cup encounter with Ross County.

This time it was 4-1 for the Celts as they marched on to the quarter-finals, with the 90th-minute strike by James Forrest meaning he has scored in each of the last 14 seasons for the Hoops.

# CELTIC TV GOAL OF THE MONTH

**July/August - Jota v Aberdeen**

# SEPTEMBER

UEFA Champions League action returned to the Celtic calendar with Group F ties against Real Madrid and Shakhtar Donetsk, but the big talking point of the month was the opening game – the first Glasgow derby of the term, and it was one that the Celts bossed from start to finish.

A win for the Ibrox side at Celtic Park would have edged them ahead in the title race, but, as it was, the resounding 4-0 victory for the Hoops took them five points clear at the top of the Premiership table as the feel-good factor increased immensely for those in green and white.

The half-time score was 3-0 but the game was put to bed a lot earlier than that as the Hoops got off on the front foot and rarely looked back, with Liel Abada opening the scoring in the eighth minute when he turned home a Matt O'Riley pass from 12 yards. And it was O'Riley who was the provider again when he put Jota through, and a delightful dink from the Portuguese Celt made it 2-0.

No guesses for who got the final touch before Abada netted his second to make it 3-0, as a sweet lay-off from O'Riley teed up the Israeli for a first-time shot into the net.

In the second half, Ibrox keeper Jon McLaughlin took up O'Riley's role as he put the ball on a plate for David Turnbull to ease it home for the fourth goal of the game.

# HOOPS HIGHPOINT

No prizes for guessing the winner this month! Aside from being a derby win, it was the only victory of a short month of football **AND** it featured the club's Goal Of The Month winner for Jota's delectable and dream-like chip for Celtic's second of the game. Aside from the above, a derby win is always going to be in the running, and a derby demolition is basically an automatic choice and some of the football on display was a joy to watch.

## CELTIC TV GOAL OF THE MONTH

### Jota v Rangers

The last of the new faces to join in the early part of the season arrived when Oliver Abildgaard signed just a few days before the derby win, and just days after taking in that spectacle, the new Bhoy also saw his team-mates welcome Real Madrid for the first time in over 40 years.

The 3-0 scoreline for the Spaniards gave no indication of Celtic's input to the game and, just a week later, that was doubly so as a 1-1 draw away to Shakhtar was scant reward for what should have been a winning performance by the Celts.

The month ended with a surprise 2-0 defeat to St Mirren in Paisley, but those points gained in the first game of September still kept the Hoops at the top of the table.

## THE GAMES

| Comp | Venue | Date | Opposition | Score | Scorers |
|------|-------|------|------------|-------|---------|
| SPFL | H | Sat 3 | Rangers | 4-0 | Abada 8, 40, Jota 32, Turnbull 79 |
| CL | H | Tue 6 | Real Madrid | 0-3 | |
| CL | A | Wed 14 | Shakhtar Donetsk | 1-1 | Bondarenko 10 og |
| SPFL | A | Sun 18 | St Mirren | 0-2 | |

## TOP OF THE TREE

| | P | W | D | L | F | A | GD | Pts |
|---|---|---|---|---|---|---|----|----|
| 1 CELTIC | 7 | 6 | 0 | 1 | 25 | 3 | 22 | 18 |
| 2 Rangers | 7 | 5 | 1 | 1 | 16 | 8 | 8 | 16 |
| 3 Hearts | 7 | 4 | 1 | 2 | 13 | 8 | 5 | 13 |

# OCTOBER

**FOLLOWING the relative inactivity of September when only four games were played, there was a flurry of nine games throughout October in three competitions as the Celts progressed to the semi-final of the League Cup and went further ahead at the top of the table despite VAR making a controversial debut in Scottish football.**

The Hoops finished with 10 men as they protected a 2-1 lead over Motherwell in the month opener, before two defeats to RB Leipzig in Europe sandwiched the most dramatic of endings to a game. In Perth, St Johnstone equalised in the 93rd minute only for Giorgos Giakoumakis to perfectly illustrate the Celtic spirit by netting a last-gasp winner in the 95th minute, just when the Saints thought they had knocked the wind out of the Celts.

James Forrest was the next to grab the glory when he netted a hat-trick in a 6-1 win over Hibernian at Celtic Park in a game that also featured a Giakoumakis double. The next display was just as dominant as the side secured a place in the League Cup semi-final at Hampden against Kilmarnock, with a 4-0 win over Motherwell at Fir Park.

Next up was Hearts at Tynecastle, and although a nail-biting 4-3 win there would be memorable under normal circumstances, the introduction of VAR to Scottish football only added to the drama.

Hearts scored twice from the spot, the first of those delivered by VAR after Celtic had an earlier 'goal' denied by the same process.

Then, in first-half time added on, what looked like a stick-on penalty for Celtic was also ignored by the VAR officials.

With the game tied at 3-3, the deadlock was broken by Greg Taylor who somehow found himself in the six-yard box to knock in the winner.

Celtic's next league game was Taylor's 100th outing for the Hoops and he was on the scoresheet once more as the 3-0 win at Livingston took the Hoops four points clear at the top.

## HOOPS HIGHPOINT

The highpoint belongs to James Forrest as, at the start of the season, he was six short of 450 games for the Hoops and just four away from netting 100 goals for the club. His hat-trick against Hibernian made him a Century Bhoy as he became only the 30th Celt to score 100 goals for the club.

## CELTIC TV GOAL OF THE MONTH

**James Forrest v Hibernian**

16

## THE GAMES

| Comp | Venue | Date | Opposition | Score | Scorers |
|------|-------|------|-----------|-------|---------|
| SPFL | H | Sat 1 | Motherwell | 2-1 | Kyogo 15, Hatate 64 |
| CL | A | Wed 5 | RB Leipzig | 1-3 | Jota 47 |
| SPFL | A | Sat 8 | St Johnstone | 2-1 | Considine og 42, Giakoumakis 90+5 |
| CL | H | Tue 11 | RB Leipzig | 0-2 | |
| SPFL | H | Sat 15 | Hibernian | 6-1 | Forrest 9, 24 & 58, Giakoumakis 18, 73, Maeda 89 |
| LC | A | Wed 19 | Motherwell | 4-0 | Abada 44, 55, Hatate 60, Kyogo 75 |
| SPFL | A | Sat 22 | Hearts | 4-3 | Forrest 14, Giakoumakis 55, Maeda 58, Taylor 76 |
| CL | H | Tue 25 | Shakhtar Donetsk | 1-1 | Giakoumakis 34 |
| SPFL | A | Sun 30 | Livingston | 3-0 | Kyogo 9, Taylor 53, Jota 87 |

## TOP OF THE TREE

| | P | W | D | L | F | A | GD | Pts |
|---|---|---|---|---|---|---|----|----|
| 1 CELTIC | 12 | 11 | 0 | 1 | 42 | 9 | 33 | 33 |
| 2 Rangers | 12 | 9 | 2 | 1 | 31 | 11 | 20 | 29 |
| 3 Hibernian | 13 | 6 | 2 | 5 | 17 | 16 | 1 | 20 |

# NOVEMBER

**CELTIC'S final Group F game in the Champions League saw the side travel to the Bernabeu to take on Real Madrid, and the current holders and 14-time winners of the trophy showed their class in a 5-1 win on their home patch.**

Following that, it was back to league business for the Celts with three games in a week before jetting to Australia to take part in the Sydney Super Cup as thousands of Celts Down Under awaited the homecoming of Ange Postecoglou with his team.

The Hoops took part in games against Sydney FC and Everton as the Aussie Hoops supporters lapped up the opportunity to see the Celts in the flesh and, although the results didn't deliver the trophy, the exercise was a success as the team, minus World Cup players Josip Juranovic, Daizen Maeda, Cameron Carter-Vickers and Aaron Mooy, got in vital game time in the sun as well as pleasing the ex-pat support.

Prior to that, though, the Celts had built up a nine-point lead at the top of the SPFL thanks to three straight victories, whilst Rangers had dropped points to both sets of Saints – a 2-1 defeat at St Johnstone and a 1-1 draw at St Mirren.

While that was going on, home games for the Hoops against Dundee United and Ross County bookended a trip to Motherwell, and those nine points gained emphasised Celtic's superiority at the top of the table.

The first game against United was tied at 2-2 going into the final minutes after the visitors had equalised in the 87th minute, but Kyogo in the 90th minute and Liel Abada just 60 seconds later typified Celtic's never-say-die attitude.

That was followed by two 2-1 wins, meaning the Celts would go into their December schedule with that nine-point cushion at the top of the league.

## CELTIC TV GOAL OF THE MONTH

**Sead Hakšabanović v Ross County**

## THE GAMES

| Comp | Venue | Date | Opposition | Score | Scorers |
|------|-------|------|-----------|-------|---------|
| CL | A | Wed 2 | Real Madrid | 1-5 | Jota 84 |
| SPFL | H | Sat 5 | Dundee United | 4-2 | Hakšabanović 6, 34, Kyogo 90, Abada 90+1 |
| SPFL | A | Wed 9 | Motherwell | 2-1 | Kyogo 15, Maeda 84 |
| SPFL | H | Sat 12 | Ross County | 2-1 | Turnbull 62, Hakšabanović 68 |
| SSC | A | Thu 17 | Sydney FC | 1-2 | Kyogo 23 |
| SSC | A | Sun 20 | Everton | 0-0 | (Lost 4-2 on pens) |

## TOP OF THE TREE

| | P | W | D | L | F | A | GD | Pts |
|---|---|---|---|---|---|---|----|-----|
| 1 CELTIC | 15 | 14 | 0 | 1 | 50 | 13 | 37 | 42 |
| 2 Rangers | 15 | 10 | 3 | 2 | 34 | 14 | 20 | 33 |
| 3 Aberdeen | 15 | 8 | 1 | 6 | 29 | 23 | 6 | 25 |

# HOOPS HIGHPOINT

Usually, a 2-1 home win over Ross County wouldn't merit such recognition, but coupled with the 1-1 draw between St Mirren and Rangers earlier that day, it meant that Celtic would go into the World Cup break a full nine points ahead at the top of the table. Such was Celtic's ongoing intent, not only did they finish November nine points in front but they also ended December, January, February and March with the same nine-point gap…before increasing that.

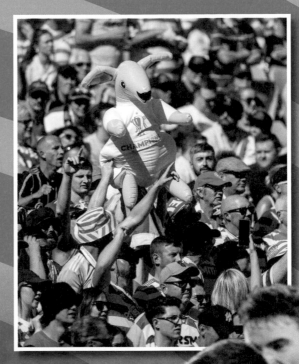

# DECEMBER

**UP until midway through the month, December had been all about the World Cup in Qatar, with the Hoops not back in action until the December 17 game against Aberdeen up at Pittodrie.**

Not that there was no direct Celtic interest in the Middle East action with no fewer than four Celts in action for their countries – Daizen Maeda with Japan, Aaron Mooy with Australia, Cameron Carter-Vickers for the USA and Croatian, Josip Juranovic.

All received rave reviews, and while all this was going on, the Celts themselves were in Portugal fine-tuning their fitness ahead of the return to action. The club were also ahead of the action in the winter transfer dealings, by snapping up Alistair Johnston from CF Montreal in Canada and Yuki Kobayashi from Japanese side Vissel Kobe.

That meant the Japanese defender was able to join up with his new team-mates in Portugal while the addition of Johnston meant there were now five Celts having a breather at the end of the World Cup, as he was representing Canada in Qatar.

Both new Bhoys were interested spectators when the Hoops took on Aberdeen at Pittodrie. And the game was notable for the return of Callum McGregor from injury, and the skipper not only completed more passes than any other player in the SPFL this season, his pass tally for the game was higher than the entire Aberdeen team.

His most important touch, though, was his 88th-minute shot that gave Celtic the vital three points in a game in which the Hoops had more possession than they did in the 9-0 win over Dundee United such was their territorial advantage.

The festive season continued in celebratory fashion as victories over Livingston, St Johnstone and Hibernian maintained Celtic's winning run until the end of the calendar year while the nine-point lead remained.

## CELTIC TV GOAL OF THE MONTH

**Daizen Maeda v Hibernian**

# HOOPS HIGHPOINT

The return to action of a player as vital as club captain Callum McGregor following injury is always a reason to celebrate, but the fact that he took the game by the scruff of the neck just three minutes from time to rattle home the winner was crucial in maintaining Celtic's gap at the top of the table. Not that it was a game of few chances, as Aberdeen didn't only park the bus, they parked two of them, took the wheels off and threw away the ignition keys in a bid to stop the Celts from scoring – they almost managed until our skipper marked his comeback in style.

## THE GAMES

| Comp | Venue | Date | Opposition | Score | Scorers |
|------|-------|------|------------|-------|---------|
| SPFL | A | Sat 17 | Aberdeen | 1-0 | McGregor 88 |
| SPFL | H | Wed 21 | Livingston | 2-1 | Obileye og 23, Kyogo 45 |
| SPFL | H | Sat 24 | St Johnstone | 4-1 | Hatate 14, 52, Kyogo 18, 40 |
| SPFL | A | Wed 28 | Hibernian | 4-0 | Mooy 28, 58 (pen), Maeda 36, Kyogo 64 |

## TOP OF THE TREE

|  | P | W | D | L | F | A | GD | Pts |
|--|---|---|---|---|---|---|----|-----|
| 1 CELTIC | 19 | 18 | 0 | 1 | 61 | 15 | 46 | 54 |
| 2 Rangers | 19 | 14 | 3 | 2 | 44 | 18 | 26 | 45 |
| 3 Hearts | 18 | 8 | 4 | 6 | 32 | 30 | 2 | 28 |

# JANUARY

THE week, the month and the year began with a trip to Ibrox, and there were two points during the game when the home fans were silenced, first in the fifth minute when Daizen Maeda put the Celts ahead, then two minutes from the end when Kyogo equalised after Rangers had gone in front with two goals either side of the break.

With home advantage, this was seen as the opportunity for the Ibrox side to cut Celtic's lead to six points, but as it was, the difference remained the same and would stay that way at the month's end. The Hoops continually increased their goal difference with no goals against in the remaining games, resulting in progress in both the League Cup and the Scottish Cup.

The League Cup saw a visit to Hampden for the semi-final against Kilmarnock and the 2-0 win paved the way for a final showdown with Rangers, while Morton visited in the Scottish Cup, with a 5-0 victory for the Hoops.

Just the week before that Kilmarnock game, the clubs also met in the SPFL and the 2-0 win at Celtic Park was perhaps an indication of the cup meeting at the National Stadium. The Hoops' next league game was welcoming the only side to have beaten them in the campaign so far – St Mirren.

There was no repeat this time, with a 4-0 win nicely increasing the goal difference further while the month was rounded off with a trip to Tannadice, and while it may not have reached the heights of the earlier 9-0 win there, the 2-0 defeat of Dundee United still kept the Celts on course.

The January transfer window also saw activity with Josip Juranovic and Giorgos Giakoumakis on their travels, whilst Alistair Johnston, Hyeongyu Oh, Tomoki Iwata and Yuki Kobayashi came in to join the ranks.

## CELTIC TV GOAL OF THE MONTH

Ben Quinn v Civil Service Strollers

# HOOPS HIGHPOINT

The entire month was a bit of a high, starting with coming away from Ibrox with a point to maintain the nine-point lead then advancement in both cup competitions and a run of clean sheets, but perhaps the highpoint was the smooth running of the transfer window. Once more, the club not only did the business early with foresight in December ensuring that Alistair Johnston was available for the derby – the very first game of the year – but the departures of fine players such as Josip Juranovic and Giorgos Giakoumakis barely registered a blip on Celtic's progress with ready-made replacements already on board.

## THE GAMES

| Comp | Venue | Date | Opposition | Score | Scorers |
|------|-------|------|------------|-------|---------|
| SPFL | A | Mon 02 | Rangers | 2-2 | Maeda 5, Kyogo 88 |
| SPFL | H | Sat 07 | Kilmarnock | 2-0 | Jota 45, Kyogo 52 |
| LC | N | Sat 14 | Kilmarnock | 2-0 | Maeda 18, Giakoumakis 90+5 |
| SPFL | H | Wed 18 | St Mirren | 4-0 | Abada 15, Kyogo 35, 53, Turnbull 86 |
| SC | H | Sat 21 | Morton | 5-0 | Mooy (pen) 18, 85, Kyogo 21, 45+1, Turnbull 42 |
| SPFL | A | Sun 29 | Dundee United | 2-0 | Jota 51, Mooy 56 |

## TOP OF THE TREE

| | P | W | D | L | F | A | GD | Pts |
|------|---|---|---|---|---|---|----|-----|
| 1 CELTIC | 23 | 21 | 1 | 1 | 71 | 17 | 54 | 64 |
| 2 Rangers | 23 | 17 | 4 | 2 | 53 | 22 | 31 | 55 |
| 3 Hearts | 23 | 11 | 6 | 6 | 42 | 31 | 11 | 39 |

# FEBRUARY

SO to the second month of the year, with progress to the Scottish Cup semi-final alongside 18 goals scored and just three going the other way, the month finished with not only a derby win at Hampden, but the **League Cup** was lifted in that game.

Two league outings started the month with full points gathered at home against Livingston then away at St Johnstone thanks to 3-0 and 4-1 wins respectively in a month in which Celtic's Japanese Bhoys shone in front of goal. Indeed, no fewer than 10 of February's 18 goals were scored by the former J.League contingent with Kyogo scoring four, Daizen Maeda netting twice and Reo Hatate also hitting the net four times with consecutive doubles against St Mirren in the Scottish Cup and Aberdeen in the league.

The big one, though, was the final game of the month, and one in which Kyogo finished off with a double and his 23rd and 24th goals of the season, as the Hoops beat Rangers 2-1 to lift their second consecutive League Cup with Ange Postecoglou now winning two out of two in the competition.

Kyogo struck first just before the break after a succession of passes from the Hoops, and little more than 10 minutes after the restart, he struck again with a similar goal at the other end of the pitch, and despite Rangers pulling one back, the Celts finished the game strongly and could have added to their score in the final minutes.

## HOOPS HIGHPOINT

What would you rather win, a derby or a cup final? The correct answer, of course, is both in the same game, and the last game of February gave the Hoops the chance to do just that, as they grabbed the opportunity, and therefore the League Cup, with both hands. The previous season, Celtic faced Hibernian in the final and won 2-1 thanks to two Kyogo goals – and this time Celtic faced Rangers in the final and won 2-1 thanks to two Kyogo goals! Ange Postecoglou retained the very first trophy he won as Hoops manager as the club celebrated winning the League Cup for the 21st time – and for the seventh time in nine seasons.

## THE GAMES

| Comp | Venue | Date | Opposition | Score | Scorers |
|------|-------|------|------------|-------|---------|
| SPFL | H | Wed 01 | Livingston | 3-0 | Taylor 29, Maeda 33, Kyogo 45+2 |
| SPFL | A | Sun 05 | St Johnstone | 4-1 | Considine og 13, Kyogo 22, Mooy 38, Turnbull 90+3 |
| SC | H | Sat 11 | St Mirren | 5-1 | Maeda 15, Hatate (pen) 76, 90+4, Oh 80, O'Riley 88 |
| SPFL | H | Sat 18 | Aberdeen | 4-0 | McGregor 2, Hatate 13, 76, Abada 89 |
| LC | N | Sun 26 | Rangers | 2-1 | Kyogo 43, 56 |

## TOP OF THE TREE

|  | P | W | D | L | F | A | GD | Pts |
|--|---|---|---|---|---|---|----|----|
| 1 CELTIC | 26 | 24 | 1 | 1 | 82 | 18 | 64 | 73 |
| 2 Rangers | 26 | 20 | 4 | 2 | 61 | 23 | 38 | 64 |
| 3 Hearts | 26 | 12 | 6 | 8 | 45 | 37 | 8 | 42 |

# CELTIC TV GOAL OF THE MONTH

Reo Hatate v St Mirren

# MARCH

**MARCH started with a visit to the only ground in Scotland where the Hoops had lost a game so far that season, but it proved to be a very satisfying journey and the Celts returned from Paisley with three points after a convincing 5-1 win.**

The Saints had earlier won 2-0 in Paisley, inflicting that solitary defeat, and another shock could have been on the cards when the home side went ahead from the spot as early as the sixth minute. However, there were five different scorers for the Celts after the break with two January signings, Alistair Johnston and Hyeongyu Oh, both netting their first goals for the club in the 5-1 win.

Then came a vital double-header against Hearts, with a potentially testing midweek league encounter at Celtic Park followed three days later with a tough trip to Tynecastle in the Scottish Cup quarter-final.

At that point, Hearts looked very safe in third position and were seen as a threat in both games, however, commanding victories for the Hoops, 3-1 in the league and 3-0 in the cup, sent the Tynecastle side into a tailspin of successive defeats that marked their season.

That left a visit by the other side from the capital, and, despite going behind, the Celts kept up their goal-scoring average with a 3-1 win over Hibs.

## CELTIC TV GOAL OF THE MONTH

### Sead Hakšabanović v Hearts

# HOOPS HIGHPOINT

During the month, the Celts recorded an aggregate score of 14-3 in four games for a very healthy return, as well as keeping up their more than impressive goal ratio in the games. That, however, doesn't tell the whole story as in each of the three games in which the Hoops lost a goal, they did so to the first goal of the game – going behind in the sixth minute of the first two and in the 39th minute of the third. The 'We Never Stop' mantra came to the fore, though, and proved that Celtic just never give up.

## THE GAMES

| Comp | Venue | Date | Opposition | Score | Scorers |
|------|-------|------|------------|-------|---------|
| SPFL | A | Sun 05 | St Mirren | 5-1 | Jota 56, Johnston 61, Abada 70, O'Riley 72, Oh (pen) 80 |
| SPFL | H | Wed 08 | Hearts | 3-1 | Maeda 25, Kyogo 60, Hakšabanović 84 |
| SC | A | Sat 11 | Hearts | 3-0 | Mooy 2, Kyogo 45, Carter-Vickers 80 |
| SPFL | H | Sat 18 | Hibernian | 3-1 | Jota (pen) 52, Oh 82, Hakšabanović 90+4 |

## TOP OF THE TREE

|   | P | W | D | L | F | A | GD | Pts |
|---|---|---|---|---|---|---|----|-----|
| 1 CELTIC | 29 | 27 | 1 | 1 | 93 | 21 | 72 | 82 |
| 2 Rangers | 29 | 23 | 4 | 2 | 72 | 27 | 45 | 73 |
| 3 Hearts | 29 | 13 | 6 | 10 | 49 | 43 | 6 | 45 |

# APRIL

AS far as months go, April was well up there as the Celts increased their lead at the top of the table from nine points to 13, increased the goal difference by four from 74 to 78 and progressed to the club's 60th Scottish Cup final.

The month started with a 2-0 win on a trip to Dingwall for the final game of the season against Ross County, as well as a visit to Kilmarnock where a 20-minute spell in the first half produced four goals in a game that was eventually won 4-1.

Those on-the-road games produced six very valuable points, however it was the weekends spent in Glasgow that produced the most telling outcomes of the month.

First of all, the final pre-split derby of the SPFL season saw the Hoops move from nine points ahead to 12 points with a thrilling 3-2 win that produced another Kyogo double against the Ibrox side.

Then, a 1-1 draw with Motherwell at Celtic Park produced some tremors, but a seismic shock reverberated back 24 hours later when, helped by a stunning goal from on-loan Celt, Liam Scales, Aberdeen beat Rangers 2-0, and the two points lost on the Saturday turned into a point gained as the Hoops went 13 points ahead.

And the month finished with a Scottish Cup semi-final that felt more like a final, as a first-half goal from Jota against Rangers was scored in a split second that summed up an entire season.

## HOOPS HIGHPOINT

Well there were two obvious highpoints – but which one to choose, the league game that put the Hoops 12 points ahead, or the Scottish Cup semi-final and the plethora of circumstances (one team on the cusp of a Treble, the other finishing trophy-less) that this entailed? Or maybe choose another Rangers game – their 2-0 loss at Pittodrie that edged the Celts 13 points ahead at the top – it's your call.

## CELTIC TV GOAL OF THE MONTH

Daniel Cummings v East Stirling

## THE GAMES

| Comp | Venue | Date | Opposition | Score | Scorers |
|------|-------|------|------------|-------|---------|
| SPFL | A | Sun 02 | Ross County | 2-0 | Jota pen 45+1, Bernabei 90+5 |
| SPFL | H | Sat 08 | Rangers | 3-2 | Kyogo 26, 62, Jota 73 |
| SPFL | A | Sun 16 | Kilmarnock | 4-1 | Kyogo 7, Maeda 12, O'Riley 18, 27 |
| SPFL | H | Sat 22 | Motherwell | 1-1 | McGregor 24 |
| SC | N | Sun 30 | Rangers | 1-0 | Jota 42 |

## TOP OF THE TREE

| | P | W | D | L | F | A | GD | Pts |
|---|---|---|---|---|---|---|----|----|
| 1 CELTIC | 33 | 30 | 2 | 1 | 103 | 25 | 78 | 92 |
| 2 Rangers | 33 | 25 | 4 | 4 | 81 | 34 | 47 | 79 |
| 3 Aberdeen | 33 | 17 | 2 | 14 | 52 | 52 | 0 | 53 |

# MAY/JUNE

**WHAT better way to start the finishing run than by winning back-to-back titles – and what better way to end it than by, not only lifting the Scottish Cup, but by sealing a world record EIGHTH Treble?**

That's exactly how the home run panned out for the Hoops with the club's 53rd title being in the bag by the very first game, when a potentially difficult trip to Tynecastle was shrugged off by a team intent on being champions and tying up the title as quickly as possible.

The coronation of the Champions was sealed in the capital as second-half goals from Kyogo and Hyeongyu Oh secured the 2-0 win that took the Hoops to an unreachable 92 points and, with only 1,400 Celtic fans being allowed inside Tynecastle, the win was still celebrated worldwide by supporters on all corners of the globe.

With the title in the bag, the Celts followed that up by the foot easing off the pedal slightly and defeats at Ibrox and Easter Road sandwiched a draw with St Mirren, who, up until this trio of games, had been the only team to defeat the Hoops.

Still, any thoughts of Aberdeen also cashing in on Celtic's post-title lethargy were cast asunder by a devastating performance on Trophy Day, as the 53rd championship win was celebrated in perfect style following a 5-0 win over the Dons.

The SPFL trophy was handed to Callum McGregor and he went through the exact same process a week later, except this time the venue was Hampden and the trophy was the Scottish Cup.

Inverness Caley Thistle were the hopefuls who lined up on the other side of the pitch, but from the moment Kyogo scored the opener with his 34th goal of the season, the destination of the trophy was in little doubt, and the world record for Trebles was in the bag.

## CELTIC TV GOAL OF THE MONTH

**Kyogo v Aberdeen (first goal)**

## THE GAMES

| Comp | Venue | Date | Opposition | Score | Scorers |
|---|---|---|---|---|---|
| **MAY** | | | | | |
| SPFL | A | Sun 07 | Hearts | 2-0 | Kyogo 67, Oh 80 |
| SPFL | A | Sat 13 | Rangers | 0-3 | |
| SPFL | H | Sat 20 | St Mirren | 2-2 | Kyogo 14, McGregor 81 |
| SPFL | A | Wed 24 | Hibernian | 2-4 | Hatate (pen) 41, Oh 58 |
| SPFL | H | Sat 27 | Aberdeen | 5-0 | Kyogo 27, 32, Starfelt 78, Oh 82, 90 |
| **JUNE** | | | | | |
| SC | N | Sun 03 | Inverness CT | 3-1 | Kyogo 37, Abada 65, Jota 90+1 |

## TOP OF THE TREE

| | P | W | D | L | F | A | GD | Pts |
|---|---|---|---|---|---|---|---|---|
| 1 CELTIC | 38 | 32 | 3 | 3 | 114 | 34 | 80 | 99 |
| 2 Rangers | 38 | 29 | 5 | 4 | 93 | 37 | 56 | 92 |
| 3 Aberdeen | 38 | 18 | 3 | 17 | 56 | 60 | -4 | 57 |

# HOOPS HIGHPOINT

Again, the choice of highs could depend on where you were when the title was sealed, the SPFL trophy was presented or the Scottish Cup was won. However, the fact that the Scottish Cup win not only delivered Celtic's 116th trophy but also that world record **EIGHTH** Treble was a definite highlight – but one that couldn't have been possible without the earlier title win or the League Cup win, or, indeed, the fight that the relentless Celts put into every single game in the three tournaments.

# SHOOTING STAR CELTS

## Celts strike nine-in-a-row in goal fest at Tannadice to produce the highest scoreline of 2022/23 AND a new SPFL away record.

CELTIC already held the SPFL's highest home scoreline with a 9-0 win over Aberdeen back in 2010, and, in the final minute, the record was nearly smashed further when David Turnbull's header bounced on the line and tantalisingly veered away from the goal rather than into it for a 10-0 win against United.

But it would have to be just the nine in the end on an afternoon when it really could have been so much more on a historic day in Dundee.

With possession stats of 76 per cent and 30 shots on goal with 13 of those on target, it's little wonder the Hoops scored so many goals, but, amazingly, just five minutes before the break it was still only 1-0 to the Celts.

**1** No.1 A defence-splitting pass from Liel Abada found Jota gliding beyond the Dundee United back-line and the Portuguese winger squared it for Kyogo. After one touch to compose himself, he then steered the ball into the bottom left corner for 1-0.

No.2 This time the Japanese internationalist smashed an outstanding long-range strike first-time into the top right corner from around 25 yards out after great pressing from O'Riley rolled the ball into the striker's path. **2**

**3** No.3 Two minutes into stoppage time and Kyogo grabbed his second hat-trick in Celtic colours, a year after his first on his first start in a 6-0 win over United's cross-street rivals, Dundee. A Celtic corner was cleared to O'Riley on the edge of the area and he played a first-time ball into the box perfectly for Abada on the right who squared to Kyogo for the easiest of tap-ins.

No.4 The Celtic fans were in full voice by this point, and in the sixth minute of stoppage time they found another level as the Celts went 4-0 in front. In similar circumstances to the third, this time Abada fed in O'Riley down the right who squared it for Jota who composed himself and tapped home from a few yards out to seal the most perfect of opening 45 minutes. **4**

32

**No.5** It didn't take long to get things going again in the second half as the 50th minute produced the fifth goal for Celtic. More incisive passing cut open the hosts' defence, as Jota slid O'Riley through on goal who was extremely unselfish to square for Abada racing in from the right to tap home.

**No.6** It was easy street for Celtic at Tannadice and on 55 minutes it was 6-0, as O'Riley's free kick fired into the wall and bounced back to Juranovic. The Croatian took aim and fired a bouncing ball into the bottom right corner.

**No.7** Every Celtic attack was producing a goal and Abada was in on the act again on 59 minutes, racing into the back post in a trademark run, latching on to Reo Hatate's low cross to get Celtic's seventh of the afternoon.

**No.8** The eighth goal wouldn't come until the 77th minute, a spell that seemed so quiet considering the rate the goals were coming previously, and it was Abada who got his own hat-trick, once again pouncing at the back post to turn in a ball played across goal from substitute Daizen Maeda.

**No.9** The floodgates opened again and four minutes later it was 9-0, with Carl Starfelt getting his second goal of the season, angling a header in off the post from a David Turnbull corner.

Just like the Aberdeen game a dozen years earlier, two Celts notched hat-tricks in the 9-0 win – Kyogo and Liel Abada against United, and Gary Hooper and Anthony Stokes against the Dons – taking the number of Celtic games featuring double hat-tricks to 18.

If Turnbull's last-minute header had gone in, the Hoops would have equalled their post-war record of 10-0 against Hamilton Accies in 1968 – but will we ever again reach the club's all-time scoring record of 11-1 against Dundee in 1895?

Here's hoping!

**MATCH FACTS**
SPFL Sunday, August 28, 2022
Tannadice Park, Dundee
**DUNDEE UNITED...0**
**CELTIC...9**
(Kyogo 15, 40, 45+2, Jota 45+6,
Abada 50, 59, 77,
Juranovic 55, Starfelt 81)

33

# PARADISE

## CALLUM McGREGOR

**POSITION:** Midfielder
**SQUAD NUMBER:** 42
**D.O.B:** 14/06/93
**BORN:** Glasgow, Scotland
**HEIGHT:** 5'10"
**SIGNED:** 07/07/09

**DEBUT:**
v KR Reykjavik (a) 1-0, (UCL) 15/07/14
**PREVIOUS CLUBS:**
Celtic Youth
(on loan at Notts County while with Celtic)

## JAMES FORREST

**POSITION:** Winger
**SQUAD NUMBER:** 49
**D.O.B:** 07/07/91
**BORN:** Prestwick, Scotland
**HEIGHT:** 5'9"
**SIGNED:** 01/07/09

**DEBUT:**
v Motherwell (h) 4-0, (SPL) 01/05/10
**PREVIOUS CLUBS:**
Celtic Youth

## DAVID TURNBULL

**POSITION:** Midfielder
**SQUAD NUMBER:** 14
**D.O.B:** 10/07/99
**BORN:** Carluke, Scotland
**HEIGHT:** 6'1"
**SIGNED:** 27/08/20

**DEBUT:**
v Ross County (a) 5-0, (SPFL) 12/09/20
**PREVIOUS CLUBS:**
Motherwell

## LIEL ABADA

**POSITION:** Winger
**SQUAD NUMBER:** 11
**D.O.B:** 03/10/01
**BORN:** Petah Tikva, Israel
**HEIGHT:** 5'5"
**SIGNED:** 14/07/21

**DEBUT:**
v FC Midtjylland (h) 1-1, (CL) 20/07/21
**PREVIOUS CLUBS:**
Maccabi Petah Tikva

# PROFILES

## KYOGO FURUHASHI

POSITION: **Forward**
SQUAD NUMBER: **8**
D.O.B: **20/01/95**
BORN: **Nara, Japan**
HEIGHT: **5'7"**
SIGNED: **16/07/21**

DEBUT:
**v Hearts (a) 1-2,
(SPFL) 31/07/21**
PREVIOUS CLUBS:
**Vissel Kobe, FC Gifu**

## ANTHONY RALSTON

POSITION: **Defender**
SQUAD NUMBER: **56**
D.O.B: **16/11/98**
BORN: **Bellshill, Scotland**
HEIGHT: **6'0"**

DEBUT:
**v St Johnstone (a) 1-2,
(SPFL) 11/05/16**
PREVIOUS CLUBS:
**Celtic Youth (on loan at Queen's
Park, Dundee United and St
Johnstone while with Celtic)**

## SCOTT BAIN

POSITION: **Goalkeeper**
SQUAD NUMBER: **29**
D.O.B: **22/11/91**
BORN: **Edinburgh, Scotland**
HEIGHT: **6'0"**
SIGNED: **31/01/18**

DEBUT:
**v Rangers (a) 3-2,
(SPFL) 11/03/18**
PREVIOUS CLUBS:
**Hibernian (loan), Dundee,
Alloa Athletic, Elgin City (loan),
Aberdeen**

## STEPHEN WELSH

POSITION: **Defender**
SQUAD NUMBER: **57**
D.O.B: **19/01/2000**
BORN: **Coatbridge, Scotland**
HEIGHT: **6'3"**
SIGNED: **01/07/18**

DEBUT:
**v Hamilton Accies (a) 4-1,
(SPFL) 02/02/20**
PREVIOUS CLUBS:
**Celtic Youth
(on loan at Greenock
Morton while with Celtic)**

# PARADISE

## GREG TAYLOR

POSITION: Defender
SQUAD NUMBER: 3
D.O.B: 05/11/1997
BORN: Greenock, Scotland
HEIGHT: 5'7"
SIGNED: 02/09/19

DEBUT:
v St Mirren (h) 2-0,
(SPFL) 30/10/19
PREVIOUS CLUBS:
Kilmarnock

## JOE HART

POSITION: Goalkeeper
SQUAD NUMBER: 1
D.O.B: 19/04/87
BORN: Shrewsbury, England
HEIGHT: 6'5"
SIGNED: 03/08/21

DEBUT:
v FK Jablonec (a) 4-2, (EL) 05/08/21
PREVIOUS CLUBS:
Tottenham Hotspur, Burnley,
West Ham (loan), Torino (loan),
Birmingham City (loan), Blackpool
(loan), Tranmere Rovers (loan),
Manchester City, Shrewsbury Town

## HYEONGYU OH

POSITION: Forward
SQUAD NUMBER: 19
D.O.B: 12/04/2001
BORN: Namyangju-si, South Korea
HEIGHT: 6'1"
SIGNED: 25/01/23

DEBUT:
v Dundee United (a) 2-0,
(SPFL) 29/01/23
PREVIOUS CLUBS:
Suwon Samsung
Bluewings, Gimcheon
Sangmu (loan)

## LIAM SCALES

POSITION: Defender
SQUAD NUMBER: 5
D.O.B: 08/08/98
BORN: Barndarrig, Ireland
HEIGHT: 6'2"
SIGNED: 27/08/21

DEBUT:
v Raith Rovers (h),
3-0 (LC) 23/09/21
PREVIOUS CLUBS:
Shamrock Rovers, UCD,
(on loan at Aberdeen
while with Celtic)

# PROFILES

## MATT O'RILEY

POSITION: **Midfielder**
SQUAD NUMBER: **33**
D.O.B: **21/11/00**
BORN: **Hounslow, England**
HEIGHT: **6'2"**
SIGNED: **21/01/22**

DEBUT:
**v Hearts (a) 2-1, (SPFL)
26/01/22**
PREVIOUS CLUBS:
**Milton Keynes Dons,
Fulham**

## DAIZEN MAEDA

POSITION: **Forward**
SQUAD NUMBER: **38**
D.O.B: **20/10/97**
BORN: **Osaka, Japan**
HEIGHT: **5'8"**
SIGNED: **01/01/22**

DEBUT:
**v Hibernian (h) 2-0,
(SPFL) 17/01/22**
PREVIOUS CLUBS:
**Yokohama F. Marinos, C.S.
Marítimo (loan), Mito Hollyhock
(loan), Matsumoto Yamaga.**

## REO HATATE

POSITION: **Midfielder**
SQUAD NUMBER: **41**
D.O.B: **21/11/97**
BORN: **Suzuka, Mie, Japan**
HEIGHT: **5'8"**
SIGNED: **01/01/22**

DEBUT:
**v Hibernian (h) 2-0,
(SPFL) 17/01/22**
PREVIOUS CLUBS:
**Kawasaki Frontale**

## BENJAMIN SIEGRIST

POSITION: **Goalkeeper**
SQUAD NUMBER: **31**
D.O.B: **31/01/92**
BORN: **Therwil, Switzerland**
HEIGHT: **6'4"**
SIGNED: **21/06/22**

DEBUT:
**v Ross County (a) 4-1,
(LC) 31/08/22**
PREVIOUS CLUBS:
**Dundee United, Vaduz, Wycombe
Wanderers (loan), Solihull Moors
(loan), Cambridge United (loan),
Burton Albion (loan), Aston Villa**

# PARADISE

## CAMERON CARTER-VICKERS

**POSITION:** Defender
**SQUAD NUMBER:** 20
**D.O.B:** 31/12/97
**BORN:** Southend-on-Sea, England
**HEIGHT:** 6'0"
**SIGNED:** 31/08/21

**DEBUT:**
v Ross County (h) 3-0 SPFL, 11/09/21
**PREVIOUS CLUBS:**
AFC Bournemouth (loan), Luton Town (loan), Stoke City (loan), Swansea City (loan), Ipswich Town (loan), Sheffield United (loan), Tottenham Hotspur

## LUIS PALMA

**POSITION:** Forward
**SQUAD NUMBER:** 7
**D.O.B:** 17/01/2000
**BORN:** La Ceiba, Honduras
**HEIGHT:** 5'10"
**SIGNED:** 30/08/23

**DEBUT:**
N/A
**PREVIOUS CLUBS:**
Aris, Real Monarchs (loan), Vida

## YUKI KOBAYASHI

**POSITION:** Defender
**SQUAD NUMBER:** 18
**D.O.B:** 18/07/2000
**BORN:** Hyogo, Japan
**HEIGHT:** 6'1"
**SIGNED:** 23/11/22

**DEBUT:**
v St Mirren (h) 4-0, (SPFL) 18/01/23
**PREVIOUS CLUBS:**
Vissel Kobe, Machida Zelvia (loan), Yokohama FC (loan)

## ALISTAIR JOHNSTON

**POSITION:** Defender
**SQUAD NUMBER:** 2
**D.O.B:** 08/10/1998
**BORN:** Vancouver, Canada
**HEIGHT:** 5'11"
**SIGNED:** 03/12/22

**DEBUT:**
v Rangers (a) 2-2, (SPFL) 02/01/23
**PREVIOUS CLUBS:**
CF Montreal, Nashville SC, Vaughan Azzurri

# PROFILES

## ALEXANDRO BERNABEI

POSITION: **Defender**
SQUAD NUMBER: **25**
D.O.B: **24/09/2000**
BORN: **Iriondo Department, Argentina**
HEIGHT: **5'5"**
SIGNED: **30/06/22**

DEBUT:
**v Dundee United (a) 9-0, (SPFL) 28/08/22**
PREVIOUS CLUBS:
**Lanus**

## ODIN THIAGO HOLM

POSITION: **Midfielder**
SQUAD NUMBER: **15**
D.O.B: **18/01/2003**
BORN: **Trondheim, Norway**
HEIGHT: **5'9"**
SIGNED: **22/06/23**

DEBUT:
**v Ross County (h) 4-2, (SPFL) 05/08/23**
PREVIOUS CLUBS:
**Vålerenga, Tiller (loan)**

## MARCO TILIO

POSITION: **Forward**
SQUAD NUMBER: **23**
D.O.B: **23/08/2001**
BORN: **Hurstville, Australia**
HEIGHT: **5'7"**
SIGNED: **30/06/23**

DEBUT:
**N/A**
PREVIOUS CLUBS:
**Melbourne City, Sydney FC**

## HYUNJUN YANG

POSITION: **Midfielder**
SQUAD NUMBER: **13**
D.O.B: **25/05/2002**
BORN: **Busan, South Korea**
HEIGHT: **5'9"**
SIGNED: **26/07/23**

DEBUT:
**v Ross County (h) 4-2, (SPFL) 05/08/23**
PREVIOUS CLUBS:
**Gangwon FC**

# PARADISE

## GUSTAF LAGERBIELKE

POSITION: Defender
SQUAD NUMBER: 4
D.O.B: 10/04/2000
BORN: Stockholm, Sweden
HEIGHT: 6'3"
SIGNED: 16/08/23

DEBUT:
v Kilmarnock (a) 0-1, (LC)
20/08/23
PREVIOUS CLUBS:
IF Elfsborg, Degerfors IF (loan),
Västerås SK, Sollentuna FK,
AIK, FC Djursholm

## TOMOKI IWATA

POSITION: Midfielder
SQUAD NUMBER: 24
D.O.B: 07/04/1997
BORN: Usa, Ōita, Japan
HEIGHT: 5'10"
SIGNED: 30/12/22

DEBUT:
v Greenock Morton (h)
5-0, (SC) 21/01/23
PREVIOUS CLUBS:
Yokohama F Marinos,
Oita Trinita

## HYEOKKYU KWON

POSITION: Midfielder
SQUAD NUMBER: 22
D.O.B: 13/03/2001
BORN: Busan, South Korea
HEIGHT: 6'3"
SIGNED: 26/07/23

DEBUT:
N/A
PREVIOUS CLUBS:
Busan IPark,
Gimcheon Sangmu

## MAIK NAWROCKI

POSITION: Defender
SQUAD NUMBER: 17
D.O.B: 07/02/2001
BORN: Bremen, Germany
HEIGHT: 6'1"
SIGNED: 26/07/23

DEBUT:
v Ross County (h) 4-2,
(SPFL) 05/08/23
PREVIOUS CLUBS:
Legia Warsaw, Warta Pozna
(loan), Werder Bremen

# PROFILES

## NAT PHILLIPS

POSITION: Defender
SQUAD NUMBER: 6
D.O.B: 21/03/1997
BORN: Bolton, England
HEIGHT: 6'3"
SIGNED: 31/08/23

DEBUT:
N/A
PREVIOUS CLUBS:
Liverpool, VfB Stuttgart
(loan), Bournemouth (loan)

## PAULO BERNARDO

POSITION: Midfielder
SQUAD NUMBER: 28
D.O.B: 24/01/2002
BORN: Almada, Portugal
HEIGHT: 5'11"
SIGNED: 31/08/23

DEBUT:
N/A
PREVIOUS CLUBS:
Benfica, Benfica B,
Paços de Ferreira (loan)

## JAMES McCARTHY

POSITION: Midfielder
SQUAD NUMBER: 16
D.O.B: 12/11/90
BORN: Glasgow, Scotland
HEIGHT: 5'11"
SIGNED: 03/08/21

DEBUT:
v Hearts (h) 3-2,
(LC) 15/08/21
PREVIOUS CLUBS:
Hamilton Accies, Wigan
Athletic, Everton, Crystal
Palace

## MIKEY JOHNSTON

POSITION: Striker
SQUAD NUMBER: 90
D.O.B: 19/04/99
BORN: Glasgow, Scotland
HEIGHT: 5' 10"

DEBUT:
v St Johnstone (h) 4-1, (SPFL)
06/05/17
PREVIOUS CLUBS:
Celtic Youth

# PARADISE PUZZLES

## SPOT THE DIFFERENCE

THERE are 10 differences between these two photographs of the Celtic Ghirls going through their warm-up routine at Hampden before winning the Scottish Cup with a 2-0 win over Rangers. The first one has been circled, but can you spot the rest?

# WHO SCORED AGAINST WHO?

Here we have 11 Celts and 11 teams – but can you link the player to the team he scored his first Celtic goal against?

Reo Hatate -------------------- [          ]          Aberdeen

Cameron Carter-Vickers--- [          ]          Kilmarnock

Liel Abada -------------------- [          ]          St Mirren

Daizen Maeda -------------- [          ]          FK Jablonec

Greg Taylor------------------ [          ]          Lille OSC

Anthony Ralston------------- [          ]          Ross County

James Forrest -------------- [          ]          FC Midtjylland

David Turnbull -------------- [          ]          KR Reykjavik

Kyogo ------------------------- [          ]          Motherwell

Matt O'Riley ----------------- [          ]          Hearts

Alistair Johnston ----------- [          ]          Hibernian

# 2022/23 QUIZ

Were you paying attention during the Treble-winning season?

01 Which three Celtic Academy graduates made their debuts during the season?                  [ 01          ]

02 How many goalkeepers did Celtic use during the season?                  [ 02          ]

03 Who scored the first goal of the term?                  [ 03          ]

04 Which Celt made the most appearances in 2022/23?                  [ 04          ]

05 And which Celt made the most starts?                  [ 05          ]

06 Who scored the final league goal of the campaign?                  [ 06          ]

07 David Turnbull, Greg Taylor, Joe Hart and Liel Abada did what during the season?                  [ 07          ]

08 Against which side did James Forrest score his 100th Celtic goal?                  [ 08          ]

09 How many players did Celtic use in all competitions?                  [ 09          ]

10 Outside of Celtic Park, at which stadium did Celtic make the most appearances?                  [ 10          ]

# THE LEAGUE CUP

## PART ONE OF THE TREBLE

**JUST 14 months earlier, Celtic had sealed the 2021/22 League Cup with a 2-1 win over Hibernian thanks in no small part to two goals by Kyogo on a memorable day at Hampden. Now, the first trophy of the 2022/23 season was up for grabs again and, once more, two goals from the Japanese marksman helped deliver another 2-1 League Cup final win, this time against Rangers.**

The short trip to Hampden began six months earlier with a lengthy jaunt to Dingwall where a 4-1 win over Ross County was followed by another four-goal performance, this time with no reply from the opposition as Motherwell were defeated 4-0 at Fir Park.

That sealed a return to Hampden for the semi-final, and Kilmarnock were disposed of 2-0 to set up a final meeting with Rangers at the National Stadium with all the usual brouhaha surrounding a Glasgow derby final.

It was a well-deserved win by the Hoops with the side dominating the early exchanges and, just before the break, Kyogo was to prove the lethal difference when Greg Taylor's pass barely eluded Daizen Maeda, but his fellow-countryman was set to pounce from six yards out to give Celtic the lead.

Not long after the turnaround, Kyogo increased the lead to 2-0 at the end of a move involving Callum McGregor, Aaron Mooy and Reo Hatate and, despite Rangers pulling one back in the 64th minute, in the final passage of the game it was the Hoops who created the better chances and passed up a couple of guilt-edged opportunities to increase their lead.

And so, Celtic's 114th trophy was lifted in what would prove to be the first part of the historic world record Treble.

# – THE 21ST WIN!

## THE ROAD TO THE FINAL

### ROUND TWO
**Wednesday, August 31, 2022**
**Global Energy Stadium, Dingwall**

ROSS COUNTY... 1
(Iacovitti 68)

CELTIC... 4
(McGregor 21, Giakoumakis 25, Maeda 73, Forrest 90)

### QUARTER-FINAL
**Wednesday, October 19, 2022**
**Fir Park, Motherwell**

MOTHERWELL... 0

CELTIC... 4
(Abada 44 & 55, Hatate 60, Kyogo 75)

### SEMI-FINAL
**Saturday, January 14, 2023**
**Hampden Park**

CELTIC... 2
(Maeda 18, Giakoumakis 90+5)

KILMARNOCK... 0

### FINAL
**Sunday, February 26, 2023, Hampden Park**

CELTIC... 2
(Kyogo 43 & 56)

RANGERS... 1
(Morelos 64)

**CELTIC:** Hart, Taylor, Johnston, Carter-Vickers, Starfelt, Mooy (O'Riley 65), Hatate (Iwata 76), McGregor, Jota (Abada 64), Maeda (Hakšabanović 84), Kyogo (Hyeongyu Oh 76).
**SUBS:** Bain, Ralston, Kobayashi, Turnbull.

# THE LEAGUE TITLE

## PART TWO OF THE TREBLE

AS the season progressed, it was more a matter of 'when' rather than 'if' Celtic lift the title, and when it came to the crunch game, there had been only one defeat – to St Mirren in Paisley, and two draws, away at Ibrox and at home to Motherwell.

As it turned out, the clinching game came just after that 1-1 draw with the Fir Park side as a potentially difficult trip to Tynecastle with very few tickets available to Celtic supporters proved to be the scenario in which Celtic would be crowned champions in the capital.

Goals by Kyogo in the 67th minute and Oh with 10 minutes to go, delivered the points needed to make the Hoops uncatchable in the chase for the title and ensured the Celts were champions once again for the second successive season.

Despite lifting the title with another four games to go, less than inspiring results against Rangers, St Mirren and Hibernian weren't the ideal preparation for the final league game of the term when third-placed Aberdeen arrived hoping to put a bit of a damper on the day the SPFL trophy was to be presented.

However, a resounding 5-0 victory ensured the day went with a bang to suit the post-match pyrotechnics as Celtic celebrated their 53rd title win and their 17th of the 2000s.

By half-time it was 2-0 thanks to Kyogo's seemingly obligatory double, and when he limped off in the 50th minute, his replacement, Oh, also added a double late in the game but only after Carl Starfelt had netted the third of the game in the 78th minute.

So the 60,000 Celtic fans who thronged inside Paradise got the perfect win to celebrate Trophy Day just a week before the Scottish Cup final – and the usual post-match celebrations from Kyogo dampened any worries that his injury would preclude him from the Hampden date.

# THE 53RD WIN!

# THE ROAD TO THE FLAG

## TITLE CLINCHER

Sunday, May 7, 2023
Tynecastle Park, Edinburgh

HEARTS... 0

CELTIC... 2

(Kyogo 67, Oh 80)

CELTIC: Hart, Ralston, Starfelt, Kobayashi, Taylor, O'Riley (Mooy 70), McGregor, Hatate (Iwata 86), Jota (Hakšabanović 80), Kyogo (Hyeongyu Oh 70), Maeda (Abada 80).

SUBS: Bain, Turnbull, Bernabei, Lawal.

## TROPHY DAY

Saturday, May 27, 2023
Celtic Park

CELTIC...5

(Kyogo 27, 32, Starfelt 78, Oh 82, 90)

ABERDEEN...0

CELTIC: Hart, Johnston (Ralston 64), Iwata, Starfelt, Taylor, O'Riley (Turnbull 79), McGregor, Hatate (Summers 79), Abada (Forrest 45), Kyogo (Hyeongyu Oh 50), Jota.

SUBS: Siegrist, Bernabei, Welsh, Vata.

# THE SCOTTISH CUP

## PART THREE OF THE TREBLE

**CELTIC** reached the Hampden showdown having scored 14 goals in their four Scottish Cup games on the way there, conceding only one at the other end, a penalty to St Mirren, and they had taken the scalps of Hearts and Rangers in the process.

They went into the game against Inverness Caley Thistle knowing that, not only would a win deliver a 41st Scottish Cup, but would also mean a world record **EIGHTH** Treble and the fifth Treble in seven years.

Such stats would have been far from the players' minds, though, as, walking out of the tunnel at the National Stadium, only winning the game set before them would be on the immediate agenda – scoring goals will bring the glory, but the glory can wait until the hard work of scoring the goals is done and dusted.

The vast majority of Hampden was draped in green and white, with the expectant Celtic masses hoping that the Scottish Cup would be draped in those very same colours come the end of the proceedings.

The Highland side had caused shocks against the Hoops in previous Scottish Cup games, but surely that wouldn't happen again, not with such an important milestone for the club at stake.

The players' resolve ensured the destination of the cup was never in much doubt as a typically lethal close-range predator strike from Kyogo tipped the balance in Celtic's favour in the 37th minute.

In the 65th minute, a very similar goal, this time from Liel Abada put Celtic 2-0 in front and, even when Caley Thistle pulled one back against the run of play in the 84th minute, there was still confidence among the green and white ranks on and off the pitch.

That was consolidated when Jota calmly netted Celtic's third of the game just as the match entered time added on, and once more the Scottish Cup had green and white ribbons flowing in the Hampden breeze as the trophy was paraded around the bowl of the stadium.

# THE ROAD TO THE FINAL

## FOURTH ROUND

Saturday, January 21, 2023, Celtic Park

CELTIC... 5

(Mooy 18 pen & 85, Kyogo 21 & 45+1, Turnbull 42)

MORTON... 0

## FIFTH ROUND

Saturday, February 11, 2023, Celtic Park

CELTIC... 5

(Maeda 15, Hatate 76 pen & 90+4, Oh 80, O'Riley 88)

ST MIRREN... 1

(O'Hara 85 pen)

## QUARTER-FINAL

Saturday, March 11, 2023, Tynecastle Park, Edinburgh

HEARTS... 0

CELTIC... 3

(Mooy 2, Kyogo 45, Carter-Vickers 80)

## SEMI-FINAL

Sunday, April 30, 2023, Hampden Park

CELTIC... 1

(Jota 42)

RANGERS... 0

## FINAL

Saturday, June 3, 2023, Hampden Park

CELTIC...3

(Kyogo 37, Abada 65, Jota 90+1)

INVERNESS CALEDONIAN THISTLE 1

(MacKay 84)

CELTIC: Hart, Johnston, Iwata, Starfelt, Taylor, O'Riley (Turnbull 76), McGregor, Hatate (Hakšabanović 76), Jota (Forrest 92), Kyogo (Hyeongyu Oh 59), Maeda (Abada 45).
SUBS: Siegrist, Bernabei, Ralston, Welsh.

# THE TREBLE BHOYS

| 1966/67 | 1968/69 | 2000/01 | 2016/17 |
|---------|---------|---------|---------|
| 2017/18 | 2018/19 | 2019/20 | 2022/23 |

**THE stats on the previous pages – 21 League Cups, 53 titles and 41 Scottish Cups – tell their own stories, and, with the European Cup added to the mix, that makes for an astounding 116 trophies won prior to the start of this season.**

That European Cup win of 1967, of course, is added to the Treble won that season, the first of Celtic's run of Trebles that was also added to last season with the world record **EIGHTH** Treble, with an astounding five of them lifted in a seven-season run.

That goes some way to highlighting just how successful and dominant the Hoops have been since Brendan Rodgers' first spell as manager with 17 out of 21 trophies won over a seven-season spell.

# PART FOUR OF THE TREBLE

The current Treble-winning Celts, though, are merely carrying on the torch that has been kept aflame by the Hoops this Millennium.

In the 2000s, Celtic have won 17 titles, 11 Scottish Cups and 11 League Cups for an incredible 39 trophies won since the turn of the century.

So Hail, Hail to the 2022/23 Treble Bhoys for keeping the run going.

# THE 8TH WIN!

# THE 1, 2, 3...FOUR!

## THE MEN WHO HAVE RAISED THE CELTIC TREBLE SILVERWARE

BIG Billy, Boydy, Broony and Calmac...no, it's not the cast members of a streetwise Scottish movie, it's the FOUR Celtic captains who have led the club to Trebles.

Billy McNeill, Tom Boyd, Scott Brown and, now, Callum McGregor are the quartet, the Fab Four who lifted the trophies during some of the greatest seasons in a history of great seasons for the men in green and white.

Cesar did it twice under Jock Stein in the 1960s, Boydy led a team under Martin O'Neill that thrilled an entirely new generation of Celtic fans who were tasting continued success basically for the first time, Broony, of course, skippered the Quadruple Treble and, one of the members of that side, Callum McGregor, went on to captain the side for the 2022/23 Treble.

### Billy McNeill (2) – 1966/67, 1968/69

The possibility of a Treble came into play in the late 1940s when the League Cup arrived on the scene, with the league and Scottish Cup Double being the top target prior to that. However, back when the Glasgow Cup and the Charity Cup were tournaments that attracted large crowds, Celtic won a Quadruple of sorts in 1907/08 when all four trophies were won. However, even that was bettered in 1966/67 when Celtic's first proper Treble was added to by the Glasgow Cup, still then a big attraction, and, of course, the crème de la crème, the European Cup. Billy McNeill was Jock Stein's commander on the pitch as the Hoops won every single competition they entered. A couple of seasons later, the Treble was lifted again and, indeed, circumstances dictated that all three trophies were lifted inside a 21-day period in April of 1969.

## Tom Boyd (1) – 2000/01

When injury forced Paul McStay to retire in 1997, Tom Boyd was ready and willing to step into the captain's boots and he did so under the most trying of circumstances – the forthcoming season was the one that Celtic had to win to stop the 10. Under Wim Jansen, the skipper led the Celts to one of the most memorable title wins ever, and, under Martin O'Neill a few seasons later he made even more history by becoming the first Celtic captain since Billy McNeill in the 1960s to lead Celtic to a Treble. The League Cup was lifted with a 3-0 win over Kilmarnock in March. Barely a week into April, the league was in the bag with another five games yet to play, and, on the final day of the season, Boydy lifted the Scottish Cup to complete the Treble.

## Scott Brown (4) – 2016/17, 2017/18, 2018/19, 2019/20

Scott Brown took up the captain's baton from Stephen McManus in 2010 and had already won no fewer than **TEN** winner's medals with the Hoops by the time his first Treble season came along. The fact that he departed four years later with a haul of 22 medals tells you what happened in the interim. The Invincible Treble was followed by the Double Treble, then the Treble Treble and, of course, the Quadruple Treble. Each achievement was as unprecedented as the next as the media ran out of superlatives to describe what was happening while Broony led the Hoops to an astounding 12 successive trophies in four seasons. We were quite used to the silverware being adorned by green and white ribbons.

## Callum McGregor (1) – 2022/23

Also taking part in the Quadruple Treble was Callum McGregor, and, when Scott Brown parted company with the club, new manager Ange Postecoglou decided that the midfielder was the ideal man to step into Broony's shoes. It was among the earliest of many shrewd and pinpoint decisions by the manager, and the Scottish Cup of 2022 was the only trophy to have slipped from their grasp in two seasons as manager and captain. Indeed, Callum McGregor is now the only player on the planet to have **FIVE** Trebles under his belt – an amazing feat.

## CELTS AROUND THE WORLD WORDSEARCH

HIDDEN in this word grid are just 20 of our far-flung Celts from around the world who made the trip to Glasgow to join the Hoops, so see how many you can find.

| | | | | | | | | | | | | | | | | | | | | | | |
|---|---|---|---|---|---|---|---|---|---|---|---|---|---|---|---|---|---|---|---|---|---|---|
| J | E | A | N | J | O | E | L | P | E | R | R | I | E | R | D | D | O | E | N | K | E | A | U | O |
| J | A | N | V | E | N | N | E | G | O | O | R | O | F | H | E | S | S | O | H | H | G | Z | A | D |
| J | I | O | O | H | N | A | V | E | R | R | E | I | P | M | R | G | D | D | C | R | I | E | M | D |
| C | C | I | C | T | F | I | C | R | I | D | A | N | A | U | E | O | A | T | A | M | B | M | A | E |
| G | I | H | A | T | E | M | A | B | D | E | L | H | A | O | M | R | A | V | I | M | D | C | Y | M |
| A | V | V | A | L | S | I | N | A | T | S | L | W | R | I | I | I | V | K | U | V | A | Y | N | B |
| M | O | U | O | P | G | E | N | T | V | E | T | G | N | U | V | A | W | O | P | I | R | K | A | T |
| V | R | G | E | K | B | F | O | H | D | N | I | S | S | S | L | K | D | S | I | C | I | N | W | H |
| I | O | D | R | Y | R | K | B | B | O | O | A | Z | K | S | A | R | H | U | U | T | U | O | R | E |
| T | T | T | R | C | L | E | A | E | R | M | W | I | I | E | E | U | G | N | U | O | S | D | O | N |
| A | S | Z | I | N | F | M | B | S | O | D | R | N | Z | I | N | A | L | D | K | R | Z | J | T | R |
| N | J | C | U | Z | E | T | A | L | O | E | A | J | R | S | Z | Y | K | H | W | W | W | I | C | I |
| O | A | A | G | T | T | M | V | W | A | T | W | R | U | I | D | S | K | U | H | A | D | O | I | K |
| D | M | T | A | W | A | F | C | H | S | Y | E | K | O | K | I | M | I | Z | U | N | O | O | V | L |
| O | L | H | Z | R | B | Z | R | Z | P | P | E | I | R | N | G | B | F | J | L | Y | W | H | D | A |
| M | E | S | I | S | Y | F | F | I | L | N | L | L | U | B | O | M | O | R | A | V | C | N | N | R |
| I | I | P | O | K | D | I | E | E | A | I | M | T | E | Y | A | L | B | E | R | K | O | A | M | S |
| S | N | P | I | J | C | U | O | K | M | O | R | T | E | N | W | I | E | G | H | O | G | V | Z | S |
| S | A | V | L | R | N | J | A | E | S | A | R | A | M | A | S | S | O | I | G | R | O | E | G | O |
| A | D | K | I | F | N | M | O | R | T | E | N | W | I | E | G | H | O | R | S | T | E | R | R | N |
| M | D | D | M | A | U | V | H | S | H | U | N | S | U | K | E | N | Y | K | A | S | A | R | E | I |
| B | A | G | E | R | C | T | B | O | K | N | E | H | C | T | A | I | V | S | K | I | R | E | C | V |
| N | M | J | A | N | V | E | N | N | E | G | O | O | R | O | F | H | E | S | S | E | L | I | N | K |
| Y | D | H | A | R | A | L | D | B | R | A | T | T | B | A | K | K | T | Y | M | J | H | P | C | N |
| J | Z | T | L | T | T | L | U | B | O | M | O | R | A | V | C | I | K | B | H | Z | P | I | W | E |

| | | | |
|---|---|---|---|
| SHUNSUKE NAKAMURA | JEAN JOEL PERRIER DOUMBE | HATEM ABD ELHAMED | LUBO MORAVCIK |
| JAN VENNEGOOR OF HESSELINK | ERIK SVIATCHENKO | MASSIMO DONATI | HENRIK LARSSON |
| PIERRE VAN HOOIJDONK | GEORGIOS SAMARAS | VICTOR WANYAMA | STANISLAV VARGA |
| MORTEN WIEGHORST | EMILIO IZAGUIRRE | HARALD BRATTBAKK | DANIEL MAJSTOROVIC |
| KOKI MIZUNO | EYAL BERKOVIC | DARIUSZ WDOWCZYK | NADIR CIFTCI |

# SPOT THE BALL

AMERICAN Celt Kit Loferski is on the attack against Glasgow City at Celtic Park. There are six match balls in this photo, but, of course, only one is the real one. Can you spot which one it is?

# MANAGEMENT MOVES

Here we have the names of some previous Celtic managers and a list of teams that they also managed. Can you link the manager to the club?

|  | |  |
|---|---|---|
| Jimmy McGrory ---- | | Brighton |
| Jimmy McStay ----- | | Birmingham City |
| Jock Stein --------- | | Coventry City |
| Billy McNeill -------- | | Lillestrøm SK |
| Davie Hay---------- | | Hamilton Accies |
| Liam Brady -------- | | Sporting Lisbon |
| Lou Macari---------- | | Kilmarnock |
| Wim Jansen -------- | | Tranmere Rovers |
| Jo Venglos--------- | | Dunfermline |
| John Barnes-------- | | Manchester City |
| Gordon Strachan-- | | KSC Lokeren |

# GHIRL POWER

**AS the season neared its end, Celtic's last three games of the term to be played in Glasgow proved that the standing of the women's game in Scotland had come on in leaps and bounds even from the previous 12 months.**

That trio of games, that included two home league games, against Glasgow City and Hearts (sandwiching a trip to the capital to play Hibernian) and the Scottish Cup final against Rangers were not only a barometer as to how thrilling the end of the women's season was, but also as a measure of the standing and pulling power of that ever-growing branch of the game we all know and love.

## SUPPORTERS RALLY AROUND THE GHIRLS

It had already been announced that the Scottish Cup semi-finals and final would go ahead at the National Stadium, and further proof of the attraction and impetus of the women's game from a Celtic angle was given when the Ghirls' final two home games in an enthralling end to the season were switched from their Excelsior Stadium base in Airdrie to Celtic Park.

And that's when record after record was broken over the course of the three matches as, with a final total of 35,881, the Ghirls played in front of almost 36,000 in the final three games to take place in Glasgow.

On Thursday, May 11, a magnificent record crowd for the Scottish women's game of 9,553 turned out and gave the Ghirls glorious backing on a memorable night as they spurred on the players and roared them on to coming back from a 1-0 deficit to an amazing 3-1 win over title rivals, Glasgow City.

Goals from Tash Flint, Claire O'Riordan and Kit Loferski marked the historic occasion in fine style as the win kept the title open, going into the final week.

They followed that up a few days later with a 2-1 win over Hibernian at Meadowbank with Loferski and O'Riordan on target again as the midweek results from the Hoops, Glasgow City and Rangers meant the title was going right down to the wire on the last day with the Celts taking on Hearts at Paradise and Ibrox hosting the other two challengers.

The permutations were many as all three teams could lift the title and any one of them could be the only side from the three not to qualify for UEFA Champions League football the following term.

That crowd record of 9,553 didn't last for long as an astounding 15,882 clicked through the turnstiles at Celtic Park to urge on the Ghirls as the two games kicked off in unison, with the trophy sitting at Hampden ready to make whatever journey the outcome required.

Sadly, we all know what happened as, with the trophy on the way to Celtic Park thanks to Caitlin Hayes and Tash Flint giving Celtic a 2-0 lead over Hearts, on the other side of the river, City scored a very late goal at Ibrox and the car carrying the trophy changed direction.

The drama didn't even stop there as an equalising Rangers 'goal' which would have ironically handed the title to Celtic was chalked off in a nail-biting climax.

Although the title was grasped from Celtic's hands, in two successive home games for the Hoops, the attendance records had been smashed as the fans turned up in their droves to urge the Celts on.

Just a week after the league climax, all eyes turned to Hampden where the Celts would face Rangers in the Scottish Cup final, with the Ghirls looking for a second successive win in the competition.

And, although the 10,446 who took in the game didn't quite match the size of the crowd at Celtic Park for the last league outing of the term, it was still a record crowd for a Women's Scottish Cup final. With the vast majority of the crowd clad in green and white, it was them who were celebrating at the end of the day as the Celts won 2-0.

So, over the course of 18 days in two games at Celtic Park and one at Hampden, nearly 36,000 watched Celtic FC Women play as both the atmosphere and the ante were upped in Scottish women's football.

# LIGHTNING STRIKES TWICE FOR THE GHIRLS

## BACK2BACK SCOTTISH CUP FINAL WINS

ON May 29, 2022, Celtic FC Women made club history as they lifted the Scottish Cup for the first time when they defeated long-time trophy-winners, Glasgow City to add to the League Cup they had already won earlier in the season.

They won it the hard way against the torch-bearers of Scottish Women's football, as the game went to extra-time with the Celts playing for over 80 minutes a player down after Jodie Bartley was sent off in a harsh decision that also saw City equalise from the spot.

That made it 2-2 and that's the way it stood until the 114th minute, just six minutes away from a penalty shoot-out, when Izzy Atkinson slotted the ball home for what proved to be the historic winner.

Back then it was branded as the Scottish Women's Cup, before, in season 2022/23, it returned as the Women's Scottish Cup with a brand new logo and even a gleaming new trophy meaning that Fran Alonso's Celts were the very last winners of the old trophy and, now, they were vying to be the very first winners of the new version of the trophy.

Not only that, in going for Back2Back Scottish Cup wins, the Ghirls would be trying to win the very first Women's Scottish Cup final to be played at the National Stadium – and they did just that by defeating arch rivals Rangers 2-0 in the Hampden finale to cap off a season in which they in particular, and the women's game in Scotland in general, took strident steps forward.

In common with the men's game, the semi-finals also went ahead at Hampden, and the semi for Celtic was no less as daunting as the final itself when the Ghirls faced off with Glasgow City. Once more, a 19th-minute goal from Tash Flint proved to be the telling difference between the sides as the Hoops made it to their second successive Scottish Cup final.

Then came the May 28 final and yet another record was smashed as the 10,446 who clicked through the turnstiles, the majority of them in the Celtic End, was the biggest ever crowd at a Women's Scottish Cup final in more than 50 years of the tournament's existence.

And what they witnessed sent the vast majority of them home happy after watching yet another green and white celebration at the National Stadium as another Hoops captain raised the silverware aloft at the end of a more than convincing win.

Flint was on scoring duty once more as a Jacynta corner caused havoc in the Rangers six-yard box before the English player pounced to steer the ball home from close range with 64 minutes on the clock.

Just three minutes later it was all but over when another Jacynta corner from the same left flank saw Irish internationalist Claire O'Riordan send a looping header over the Rangers back-line to make it 2-0.

That was the way it stood at the end, and, for the second successive season, skipper Kelly Clark lifted the Scottish Cup for Celtic, but this time amid a cauldron of noise from thousands of cheering Hoops supporters.

# THE ROAD TO THE FINAL

## FOURTH ROUND
**Sunday, January 8, 2023, Falkirk Stadium, Falkirk**

FALKIRK… 0

CELTIC… 9

(Ross 5, Gallacher 22, 38, 89, O'Riordan 25, 32, Menglu 56, Hayes 68, McAneny 82)

## FIFTH ROUND
**Sunday, February 12, 2023, Meadowbank Sports Centre, Edinburgh**

BOROUGHMUIR THISTLE…0

CELTIC…5

(Bowie 1, Craig 18, 64, McAneny 32, Fergusson 86)

## QUARTER-FINAL
**Sunday, 19 March, 2023, The Oriam, Edinburgh**

HEARTS… 1

(Forsyth 15)

CELTIC… 5

(Kerner 54, O'Riordan 57, Menglu 78, Craig 86, Flint 90+1)

## SEMI-FINAL
**Sunday, April 23, 2023, Hampden Park**

CELTIC… 1

(Flint 19)

GLASGOW CITY… 0

## FINAL
**Sunday, May 28, 2023
Hampden Park**

CELTIC…2

(Flint 64, O'Riordan 67)

RANGERS…0

**CELTIC:** Tajonar, O'Riordan, Craig, Gallacher (Otto 73), Jacynta (Fergusson 87), Shen, Clark, Hayes, Flint (Goldie 87), Menglu (Bowie 87), McAneny (Loferski 56).
**SUBS:** Logan, Cusack, Barclay, Sharkey.

# SILVER CELTS SEAL
## YOUNG HOOPS IN HIGH-SCORING CUP WINS

ONE game finished as an 11-goal thriller with 6-5 being the final score, the other saw 13 goals scored, although seven of those came from the spot in a shoot-out following a 3-3 extra-time draw with the spot-kicks finishing 4-3 – but both were finals and both saw young Celtic teams triumph over their Ibrox rivals to deliver even more 2022/23 silverware to the Paradise trophy cabinet.

First up was the Youth Cup final with the under-18s travelling to Hampden to take on their Ibrox counterparts and hoping to lift the trophy for a record 16th time.

Rangers took the lead in the 19th minute before Mitchel Frame equalised and Corey Thomson gave Celtic the lead. Just six minutes later, the opposition equalised and just two minutes after that, Daniel Kelly put the young Hoops ahead again.

However, just a minute before the break, Rangers struck again and it was 3-3 at half-time as play swung from end to end in the National Stadium.

Rangers took the lead from the spot in the 52nd minute before they levelled the game by netting an own goal on the hour mark.

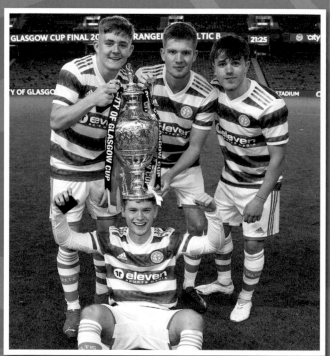

The 90 minutes finished at 4-4 and further goals from Daniel Cummings in the 96th minute and Lewis Dobbie gave the Hoops a 6-4 lead with eight minutes of the 120 left, but there was still more drama to unfold as Rangers pulled one back in time added on, but the young Celts held out for a historic and epic 6-5 win to lift the Youth Cup at Hampden.

Just a week after the under-18 triumph, the B team travelled to Ibrox to battle it out in the Glasgow Cup final, and this time there would be no extra-time, if the teams were level after 90 minutes then it would go straight to penalties.

# DERBY DOUBLE

## SCOTTISH YOUTH CUP

**Wednesday, May 3, 2023, Hampden Park**

**CELTIC... 6**

(Frame 25, Thomson 27, Kelly 35, Grant (og) 60, Cummings 96, Dobbie 112)

**RANGERS... 5**

(Roberts 19 & 33, Stevens 44, Curtis 52 (pen), Pasnik 120+1)

**After extra-time**

**CELTIC: Meikle (Gill 46), Dede (Luyeye 78), Mackenzie, Agbaire, Robertson, Ure, Hatton (Dobbie 70), Kelly, Cummings (Turley 108), Thomson (Haddow 86), Frame (Bonnar 86).**

**SUBS: Davidson.**

And another end-to-end goalscoring derby it would be as the sides regularly swapped attacking threats, evoking memories of 6-5 head-to-head by the Under-18s in the Youth Cup final.

There may not have been as many goals but it was no less exciting as the earlier game, as Adam Brooks fired the Hoops into a two-goal lead with counters in the 24th and 32nd minutes before Rocco Vata put it seemingly out of Rangers' reach with a third goal to make it 3-0 by the 36th minute.

However, the home side pulled one back before the break and made it 3-2 soon after the restart. Then, with only two minutes left on the clock, they made it 3-3 and the game went to spot-kicks.

It was a breathtaking stand-off filled with ups and downs, and after no fewer than 14 spot kicks, the two sides were finally separated as Corey Thomson stepped up and slotted home his penalty to lift the trophy for Celtic.

The undeniable hero of the shoot-out, though, was Hoops goalkeeper Josh Clarke, who saved a total of **FOUR** penalties to help Celtic to victory.

Within a week two teams of young Celts had delivered two more coveted pieces of silverware to the Paradise trophy room.

## GLASGOW CUP

**Wednesday, May 10, 2023, Ibrox Stadium**

**RANGERS... 3**

(Lowry 39, Lovelace 48, Weston 88)

**CELTIC... 3**

(Brooks 24 & 32, Vata 36)

**Celtic win 4-3 on penalties**

**CELTIC: Clarke, McPherson, Anderson, Lawal, Robertson (Corr 46), Carse, Vata (Davidson 73), Letsosa, Brooks (Kelly 84), Summers, Mackenzie (Thomson 65).**

**SUBS: Morrison, Ure, Quinn.**

# PARADISE PUZZLES

## PAGE 42: SPOT THE DIFFERENCE

## PAGE 43: WHO SCORED AGAINST WHO?

| SCORER | OPPOSITION |
| --- | --- |
| Reo Hatate | Hearts |
| Cameron Carter-Vickers | Ross County |
| Liel Abada | FC Midtjylland |
| Daizen Maeda | Hibernian |
| Greg Taylor | KR Reykjavik |
| Anthony Ralston | Kilmarnock |
| James Forrest | Motherwell |
| David Turnbull | Lille OSC |
| Kyogo | FK Jablonec |
| Matt O'Riley | Aberdeen |
| Alistair Johnston | St Mirren |

## PAGE 43: 2022/23 QUIZ

ANSWERS:

1  Rocco Vata, Ben Summers and Bosun Lawal.

2  Three – Joe Hart, Scott Bain and Ben Siegrist.

3  Stephen Welsh against Aberdeen.

4  Matt O'Riley with 52 in all – 41 starts and 11 sub appearances.

5  Joe Hart with 50.

6  Oh in the final minute of the 5-0 Trophy Day win over Aberdeen.

7  They all breached the 100-game tally for Celtic.

8  Hibernian, it was the last goal of his hat-trick against them.

9  32.

10 Hampden – two finals and two semi-finals.